LEXINGTON HERALD-LEADER

# Flavors *of* Kentucky

*A look at Kentucky's foodways including recipes that have graced
the tables at horse farm mansions, won awards for creative cooks,
and are favorite dishes at church potlucks or family reunions.*

## by sharon thompson

### photography by mark cornelison

Published by McClanahan Publishing House, Inc.

Copyright © 2006 by *Lexington Herald-Leader*

**10-digit International Standard Book Number**  0-913383-94-5
**13-digit International Standard Book Number**  978-0-913383-94-0
**Library of Congress Card Catalog Number**  2006929107

Recipes compiled by Sharon Thompson,
        Food Editor, *Lexington Herald-Leader*
Photographs by Mark Cornelison

Cover and Book Design by Kim Coleman
Copy editing by Mary Sondergard
Layout by James Asher

Manufactured in China

All book order correspondence should be addressed to:

McClanahan Publishing House, Inc.
P.O. Box 100
Kuttawa, KY  42055

270-388-9388
800-544-6959
270-388-6186 FAX

www.kybooks.com
books@kybooks.com

## special thanks

The beautiful photographs in this book wouldn't have been possible without the people who allowed us to set up our cameras in their homes, farms, restaurants and businesses. Our thanks go to:

Reba and Paul Browning, owners of Browning's Country Hams in Paris

Marilyn Campbell and her father, Harry, owners of Campbell's in Paris

Joe Castro and Brian Logsdon, chefs at The Brown Hotel in Louisville

A.J. Caudill, executive chef at Boone Tavern in Berea

Karl Crase, owner of Hall's on the River in Clark County

Gayle Deaton and James Hurm, owners of Phoebe's on Main in Beattyville

Leo and Jean Patches Keene, owners of Blue Moon Farm in Madison County

Larry Kezele, owner of Ruth Hunt Candy Co. in Mount Sterling

Jonathan Lundy, owner of Jonathan's at Gratz Park in Lexington

Steve and Anne Muntz, owners of Firefly Farm in Montgomery County

Barbara Napier, owner of Snug Hollow Farm in Estill County

Rory Snowden, owner of Tobago Ribs in Lexington

Howard Snyder, co-owner of a farm on Old Richmond Road in Fayette County

Kevin Toyoda, executive chef at Bella Notte in Lexington

Additionally, we'd like to thank Murphy's Camera of Lexington for the use of specialized photographic equipment.

# acknowledgements

Thank you to my husband, Bob, for his support, patience and his suggestions for eating out after a marathon day of cooking.

A special thank-you to my daughter Sarah Holleran for her willingness to run errands with two babies in tow.

A big thanks to my daughter Emily Chambers for helping declutter my kitchen after a day of photo shoots.

Many thanks to my sons-in-law, Eric Chambers and Bill Holleran, for their generous compliments and willingness to eat lots of leftovers.

A million thanks to photographer Mark Cornelison for reminding me that an uninspiring casserole "is what it is."

Much appreciation goes to graphics designer Kim Coleman for her extraordinary creativity.

Thank you, Mary Sondergard, for your editing expertise.

Thanks to editors Kim Parson, Sharon Ruble, Ron Garrison, Sally Scherer and Scott Shive, and to co-workers for their confidence and enthusiasm.

# contents

# introduction

## *kentucky's food traditions*

*Years ago, burgoo was cooked outdoors in large cast-iron kettles at country fairs, political meetings and church gatherings. Ingredients were a little bit of everything ... vegetables from the garden, home-canned produce and the bounty from a day of hunting. This photograph was taken at a farm on Old Richmond Road in Fayette County.*

Kentucky has a few foods you can find only in the Bluegrass State, but any food that's considered Southern is a part of Kentucky's food traditions.

The mountains of Eastern Kentucky have produced a tradition that's not really Southern. Southern food encompasses African-American, Cajun and coastal, while mountain food stems from resourceful cooks who raised much of what they ate in a severe mountain landscape. Pork, tomatoes, nuts, apples, beans, corn and potatoes are the basis from which new recipes emerged.

Western Kentucky's most famous foods are barbecued pork and fried catfish. The secret to good barbecue is to cook it low and slow, and the trick to great catfish is a good batter.

Hot Browns, fried banana peppers, beer cheese, Kentucky spoonfish caviar and Kern's Derby Pie are identified only with Kentucky, but the state is a leading producer of pork, lamb, goat and beef, and the long growing season produces an abundance of fresh fruit and vegetables.

Generations of families raised pigs, cows, chickens and sheep for food, and they fished in streams and lakes. Tobacco often supplemented their incomes.

Today, many farmers use their land to raise buffalo

*Georgia might be better known for its peaches, but Kentucky's burgeoning crop can hold its own. Using the juicy fruit for peach butter or preserves allows its sweetness to linger long after summer is gone.*

*The dining room at the nearly 100-year-old Boone Tavern in Berea is known for its traditional Southern fare. A must-have on the menu is its spoon bread, which has given rise to an annual three-day festival in mid-September.*

and goats for new markets. Those with ponds raise shrimp, trout, tilapia, catfish and spoonfish.

Orchards, pumpkin patches and vineyards are becoming "fun farms" where city folks go to catch a glimpse of country life.

Kentucky wines and paddlefish caviar are making headway in the gourmet food industry, as are small-batch bourbons and handcrafted salsas, jams and pickles.

In *Flavors of Kentucky*, we're looking at Kentucky's foodways and including recipes that have graced the tables at horse farm mansions, won awards for creative cooks, and are favorites at church potlucks and family reunions.

# appetizers

*Although Kentucky has no strong appetizer tradition, dips and spreads have been popular throughout the commonwealth's history. We're best known for heartier bar fare — beer cheese and fried banana peppers — than fancy hors d'oeuvres.*

# spinach 'n' ham herb spread

*Karin and Drew Rasmussen, owners of Herb'n Renewal, have been blending herb seasonings since 1997. They have a commercial manufacturing facility on their farm in northern Garrard County. Their seasonings, available at grocery stores and specialty markets, take the guesswork out of creating recipes. This is a recipe Karin created using their original seasoning mix.*

10-ounce package frozen spinach,
   thawed and drained
1 cup mayonnaise
1 cup sour cream
8 ounces cream cheese, softened
2 tablespoons Rub'n Season Herb'n All
1 cup diced red onion
1/2 pound thinly sliced ham, chopped

Pat or squeeze the spinach until it is dry. Combine the mayonnaise and sour cream. Add cream cheese to mayonnaise mixture and beat until smooth. Add seasoning blend and mix well. Add onion, drained spinach and ham; stir well. Cover and refrigerate overnight. Serve with assorted crackers.

# benedictine sandwich spread

*One of Louisville's most famous caterers was Jennie Benedict, who created a cucumber spread that bears her name. The spread is available in retail markets, and Benedictine recipes appear in dozens of community cookbooks. The recipe that appeared in Out of Kentucky Kitchens said, "Miss Jennie used mayonnaise made of lemon juice, real olive oil and egg yolks."*

Two 3-ounce packages cream cheese, softened

1 medium cucumber

1 onion, grated

Dash of Tabasco sauce

1 teaspoon salt

Mayonnaise

2 or 3 drops green food coloring

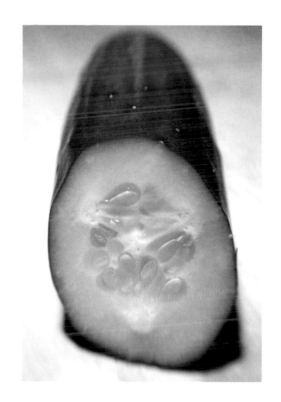

Mash the cream cheese with a fork. Peel the cucumber and grate. Extract the juice by placing the pulp in a napkin and squeezing the pulp fairly dry. Add the cucumber pulp to cream cheese. Add the onion, Tabasco sauce, salt and enough mayonnaise to make a smooth filling that can be spread easily. Add just enough green food coloring to give it a faint green tinge. Serve as a spread for tea sandwiches.

# deviled eggs

*Kentucky's first appetizer was probably the deviled egg.*

*It's the perfect size for popping into the mouth while the cook's back is turned.*

*The deviled egg - or stuffed egg - is always at family reunions, church suppers, neighborhood picnics and funeral meals. Unlike foods you can buy already prepared, the deviled egg has to be homemade to be good. Many Kentuckians flavor the yolks with mayonnaise, mustard, salt and pepper. Pickle juice, diced olives and minced country ham are common additions.*

12 hard-boiled eggs, peeled

1/2 cup mayonnaise

Salt and pepper to taste

2 teaspoons prepared mustard

1/2 cup chopped olives or sweet pickle relish

Smoked paprika for garnish

Slice the eggs in half lengthwise. Remove the yolks. Place the egg whites on a platter. Mash the yolks in a bowl with a fork. Add mayonnaise to moisten yolks and season with salt, pepper and mustard. Add the chopped olives or pickle relish and mix until light and fluffy. Spoon the mixture into egg white halves. Sprinkle with the paprika. Refrigerate until ready to serve. Makes 24 halves.

# cheese straws

*When Kentucky's horse people entertained at luncheons or tea, dishes were always made by the hostess or family cook. Cheese straws, or wafers, were a delicate savory that welcomed guests upon arrival.*

1/2 pound unsalted butter

2 cups all-purpose flour

1/2 pound sharp Cheddar cheese, grated

Dash of cayenne pepper

1 egg, well-beaten

Preheat the oven to 350 degrees. Cut the butter into flour using a pastry blender. Add the cheese and cayenne pepper and mix well. Roll the dough out on a floured board until rather thin. Cut into circles using a small biscuit cutter. Place on a cookie sheet lined with parchment paper. Brush tops with beaten egg. Bake for 10 to 15 minutes. Makes about 60 wafers.

# country ham sauce

*Silver platters piled high with country ham on tiny biscuits are on almost every Derby party table in the Bluegrass.*

*Old ham on beaten biscuits is a Kentucky tradition that has become a rare treat. Today's country ham is cured for about nine months instead of two years, and the crumbly beaten biscuits have been replaced with soft and fluffy biscuits that are ready in minutes.*

*The modern-day version of this popular party food doesn't even come close to the taste of old ham on beaten biscuits. A really good beaten biscuit is dry, crumbly and bland, which complements the strong salty taste of an old country ham.*

*Kentucky has many ham producers that package country ham, sliced and ready to go on a biscuit that you pick up in the frozen food case. If you want to jazz up your already-prepared party fare, simply brush the biscuits with a mixture of butter, bourbon, honey and mustard.*

1 pound unsalted butter,
   at room temperature

1/4 cup sweet mustard

1/2 cup honey

1/4 cup bourbon

After slicing a cooked country ham for biscuits, use the scraps to make a tasty spread. It can be served on crackers, in cream puffs for an appetizer or spooned into cherry tomatoes that have been quartered but not cut entirely through.

*The old-fashioned way to cure hams involved hanging them in smokehouses for months. The longer a ham hung, the tastier it became.*

# country ham salad spread

*After slicing a cooked country ham for biscuits, use the scraps to make a tasty spread. It can be served on crackers, in cream puffs for an appetizer or spooned into cherry tomatoes that have been quartered but not cut entirely through.*

2 cups finely ground country ham

2 cups finely diced celery

1/2 cup mayonnaise

1/4 teaspoon freshly ground black pepper

1/4 cup minced green bell pepper

1/4 cup coarsely ground pecans

1/4 cup minced onion

Combine the ham, celery and mayonnaise in a bowl. Cover and chill thoroughly. Add the black pepper, bell pepper, pecans and onion just before serving and mix well. Makes 6 to 8 servings.

# bread-and-butter pickles

*My dad's vegetable gardens often took up about 1/4 acre of our back yard and the field across the road from our house. He planted pickling cucumbers so Mom could make bread-and-butter pickles. Her recipe was never written down; she just knew how to make pickles, and she made them until all the cucumbers were gone.*

*Here's a recipe from the experts, the county extension agents, for making pickles that I followed the first few times I made pickles.*

2 1/2 pounds pickling cucumbers, sliced 1/4 inch thick

1 pound red onions, 2 to 2 1/2 inches in diameter, sliced 1/4 inch thick

3 tablespoons salt

2 cups white vinegar

2 cups sugar

1 tablespoon mustard seeds

1 teaspoon red pepper flakes

3/4 teaspoon celery seeds

3/4 teaspoon ground turmeric

1/4 teaspoon ground cloves

Combine the cucumbers, onions and salt in a large bowl and mix well. Cover with a clean wet towel and top with 2 inches of ice. Refrigerate for 3 to 4 hours. Discard the ice; drain, rinse and drain again. Combine the vinegar, sugar, mustard seeds, pepper flakes, celery seeds, turmeric and cloves in a 4-quart saucepan. Stir until sugar is dissolved. Cook, uncovered, on medium-high heat until the syrup boils.

Add the cucumbers and onions, stir to mix and heat until the syrup just begins to boil again. Pack the hot slices into sterile hot pint jars using a slotted spoon. Add the hot syrup, leaving 1/2 inch headspace. Release any air and seal each jar. Place the jars on the rack of a canner filled with hot water. Add more boiling water, if needed, so the water level is at least 1 inch above jar tops. Process for 10 minutes. Makes about five 1-pint jars.

# breads

*Homemade breads are the pride of many cooks. Long before biscuits popped out of a can, cooks could whip up a batch of biscuits before the barnyard rooster crowed.*

*Recipes for yeast rolls are a dime a dozen, but it's not the recipe that's treasured, it's the technique. Experienced bread makers can stick a finger in a bowl of warm water and tell whether it's too warm or too cool to percolate the yeast.*

*Even if we never make homemade bread, having those yeast roll recipes in our files is a priceless treasure.*

# beaten biscuits

Beaten biscuits are still made in Central Kentucky by Jackson Biscuit Co. in Winchester and Irene's Beaten Biscuits in Paris. They are "a rough form of puff pastry," Judy Jackson said. Up close, you can see the tiny layers.

The biscuits are hand-cut from a dough made with flour, sugar, salt, baking powder and lard. They are beaten to push out all the air. Early American settlers would place the dough on a hard wooden surface and beat it with the flat side of an ax, mallet, rolling pin or the heel of the hand. Later, enterprising cooks developed the beaten biscuit machine, which has been called the Southern version of a hand-cranked Italian pasta machine.

Harry Campbell of Paris, at right, makes the biscuits using an old-fashioned beaten biscuit brake, and the biscuits are sold at specialty food markets.

Beaten biscuits are eaten almost exclusively with country ham. If you would like to make beaten biscuits at home, here's a recipe using a food processor. It's from *Charles Patteson's Kentucky Cooking*.

4 cups all-purpose flour
1/2 teaspoon salt
Pinch of baking soda
1/2 teaspoon sugar
3/4 cup lard
1/2 cup cold milk
1/2 cup cold water

Place the dry ingredients in a food processor and pulse a few times to blend. Add the lard and pulse until the mixture resembles coarse meal. Add the milk and water and process for about 2 minutes or until the dough is shiny, elastic and rather sticky.

Preheat the oven to 350 degrees. Roll out on a heavily floured surface until 1/2-inch thick. Cut using a small round biscuit cutter. Prick each biscuit with three rows of holes using the tines of a fork. Place the biscuits on an ungreased cookie sheet and bake for about 10 minutes or until risen. Increase the temperature to 400 degrees and bake for 15 minutes or until slightly brown. Makes about 4 dozen.

# whipping cream biscuits

*Long before baking mixes were invented, biscuits were considered Kentucky's quick bread. We connect biscuits with so many of our favorite foods — biscuits and gravy, fried chicken and biscuits, biscuits and jelly, sausage biscuits and, of course country ham and biscuits.*

*The simplest way to make homemade biscuits is to combine two ingredients.*

1 3/4 cups self-rising flour
1/2 pint whipping cream

Combine the flour and whipping cream in a large bowl. Place the dough on a floured surface and knead for 1 to 2 minutes. Roll out dough until it is 1/2 to 3/4 inch thick. Cut with a biscuit cutter. Place the biscuits on an ungreased cookie sheet and bake at 450 degrees for 12 to 15 minutes. Makes about a dozen biscuits.

# sweet potato biscuits

*Mark Sohn, a professor at Pikeville College, has written several books on Appalachian foods. He describes sweet potato biscuits as "classic mountain, country to the core."*

*"The recipe is simple, and if you do as most mountain cooks and use self-rising flour, you can make them with three ingredients: 1/4 cup butter, 1 cup leftover sweet potato casserole and 1 cup self-rising flour."*

*If you don't have leftover sweet potato casserole, simply doctor mashed sweet potatoes like we did.*

4 cups fully cooked and mashed
   sweet potatoes
1/4 cup orange juice
1/4 cup brown sugar
1/2 teaspoon salt
1/4 teaspoon mace
1/4 teaspoon cinnamon
2 cup self-rising flour
1 cup plus 3 tablespoons butter

Preheat the oven to 400 degrees. Combine the sweet potatoes, orange juice, brown sugar, salt, mace and cinnamon in a bowl; set aside. Blend the flour with 1 cup of the butter in a separate bowl. Add the sweet potato mixture and mix. Knead and pat out to 3/4-inch thickness. Cut into 2-inch round biscuits.

Melt the 3 tablespoons butter in an 8x8-inch baking dish and add the biscuits. Bake for 12 to 15 minutes or until the biscuits are brown on the edge. Makes 9 biscuits.

This recipe was adapted from Sohn's book, *Mountain Country Cooking*.

# yeast rolls

*The aroma of freshly baked yeast rolls is as comforting as the arms of your grandmother.*

*Mass-produced yeast rolls that we take out of a bag and bake are awesome, but there's no comparison to the real thing.*

*Cooks who can make light, fluffy yeast rolls often are idolized.*

*One of those cooks was the late Thelma Linton, who was known for many years as "the best cook in Harrodsburg." She got that title in 1977 when a food writer for the Los Angeles Times visited Shakertown and heard about Linton's reputation. The writer said that every time she asked who in the area made the best rolls, the best corn pudding and the best cakes, and who was the best cook in the county, the answer was always the same: Thelma Linton.*

*Here is the recipe for Linton's famous rolls.*

## THELMA'S ROLLS

2 cups water

Pinch of sugar

Four 1/4-ounce packages rapid-rise yeast

4 eggs

2 sticks butter

1 cup Crisco

2 teaspoons salt

Not quite 2 cups sugar

2 cups boiling water

16 cups White Lily all-purpose flour

Melted butter

Heat the 2 cups of water to about 110 degrees in a saucepan. Pour the water into a bowl with the sugar. Add the yeast and stir for about 1 minute or until the yeast is dissolved and bubbles up. Beat the eggs, using an electric mixer, in a separate bowl for about 5 minutes or until they are stiff. Combine the 2 sticks butter, Crisco, salt and sugar in a separate bowl. Beat, using an electric mixer at medium speed, for about 3 to 5 minutes or until the mixture gets really creamy. Turn the mixer to low speed and add the boiling water. Turn the mixer to a slightly higher speed and add the stiff eggs and mix well. Add the yeast mixture, turn the mixer to a higher speed and mix for 30 seconds to one minute.

Sift the flour onto a piece of waxed paper or aluminum foil. Add 4 cups to the yeast mixture and mix by hand, vigorously, for 2 minutes or until the flour is well-blended. Add the remaining flour, 4 cups at a time, beating vigorously by hand for 2 minutes or so after each addition. Beat the dough well, scraping it up from the bottom of the bowl with a spatula with one hand while rotating the bowl with the other hand.

Brush the top of the dough with softened or melted butter or margarine. Cover the bowl well with foil and let it sit for several hours or until the dough has doubled in size. Place the dough in the refrigerator overnight.

Remove from the refrigerator. Melt 3 or 4 sticks of margarine or butter in a saucepan and set aside. Take out about 1/5 of the dough and knead it with as little flour as possible. Don't bear down on the dough. Knead it gently and quickly. Roll the dough out to 1/2-inch thickness and cut with a biscuit cutter. Grease the bottom of a 9-inch pan with the melted butter. Dip each roll in the remaining melted butter. Place it in the pan so it lightly touches the other rolls. Roll out the remaining dough. Let the rolls sit in the pans for about 3 hours while they rise. Bake at 375 degrees for 15 minutes. Makes 16 to 17 dozen, depending on the activity of the yeast, the eggs, the thickness of the dough and the size of the biscuit cutter. Rolls may be frozen after baking.

# hush puppies

*Hush puppies and fried catfish are traditional Friday night fare at hometown restaurants, church suppers and fund-raising events.*

*Hush puppies are basically round corn bread that is fried along with the catfish.*

*This recipe appeared on the back of Weisenberger Mills' cornmeal bags from the 1950s until 1979. The Midway company, which has been in business since 1872, has developed mixes to make hush puppies, pancakes, biscuits, corn muffins, spoon bread and pizza dough.*

2 cups cornmeal

1/4 cup all-purpose flour

1/2 teaspoon baking soda

1 teaspoon baking powder

1 teaspoon salt

1 teaspoon sugar

1/2 onion, chopped

1 cup buttermilk

1 egg, beaten

Combine the dry ingredients in a bowl. Add the onion, buttermilk and egg and mix well. Drop the batter into hot grease using a spoon. Fry until golden brown.

Note: You may substitute regular milk for buttermilk but you must omit the sugar.

# southern spoon bread

Spoon bread, a cross between pudding and wet corn bread, is one of the classic Southern breads made with cornmeal. It's one of the signature dishes on the menu at the historic Boone Tavern in Berea. Weisenberger Mills in Midway makes a spoon bread mix that's a favorite with busy cooks.

This recipe is from Look No Further by Richard T. Hougen, who was the chef at Boone Tavern in Berea for many years.

3 cups milk

1 1/4 cups white cornmeal

3 eggs, well-beaten

1 teaspoon salt

1 3/4 teaspoons baking powder

2 tablespoons butter, melted

Bring the milk to a boil in a saucepan. Stir the cornmeal into the rapidly boiling milk. Cook until very thick, stirring constantly to prevent scorching. Remove the mixture from the heat and allow it to become cold and very stiff. Add the eggs, salt, baking powder and butter. Beat using an electric mixer for 15 minutes.

Break the hardened cornmeal into the beaten eggs in small amounts, if beating by hand, until all of it is mixed in. Add the remaining ingredients and beat for 10 minutes using a wooden spoon.

Pour the mixture into a well-greased 2-quart casserole. Bake for 30 minutes at 375 degrees. Serve from the casserole dish by spoonfuls.

# corn bread

*Inexpensive, and readily available, cornmeal has kept many a Kentucky family fed during hard times. Hot bread was made simply by mixing cornmeal with a little hot water, then frying it on a griddle. When times were better, the addition of eggs and buttermilk made a more substantial bread.*

*"To make a pan of real corn bread, you have to have a good cast-iron skillet," says Ronni Lundy, a Corbin native and author of several cookbooks about Southern cooking, including Shuck Beans, Stack Cakes and Honest Fried Chicken and Butter Beans to Blackberries. "An old, well-seasoned and well-used cast-iron skillet is best," she says. "It might look greasy and caked-up on the outside, but that just means you'll get a better crust."*

*Mountain people prefer white cornmeal because it has a sharper taste and a more tender texture.*

2 to 3 tablespoons bacon drippings

2 cups cornmeal

Pinch of baking soda

Pinch of baking powder

Pinch of salt

1 egg

1 1/2 cups milk or buttermilk

Preheat the oven to 450 degrees. Pour the bacon drippings into a skillet and place in the oven. Combine the cornmeal, baking soda, baking powder and salt in a large bowl. Add the egg and milk and stir.

Remove the skillet from the oven and swirl it so it is coated with drippings. The grease should crackle and pop.

Pour the grease into the batter, mix it in quickly and pour the batter back into the skillet. Bake for 20 to 25 minutes.

"While you're waiting, you're going to start to smell that sweet, buttery scent of the corn, the seductive saltiness of the bacon grease," Lundy says. "When you pull the skillet out of the oven, the corn bread will have a glistening, golden-brown crust that will crack crisply as you cut the first slice. And when you pull that first wedge out of the pan, a little cloud of corn-sweet steam will rise up in your face."

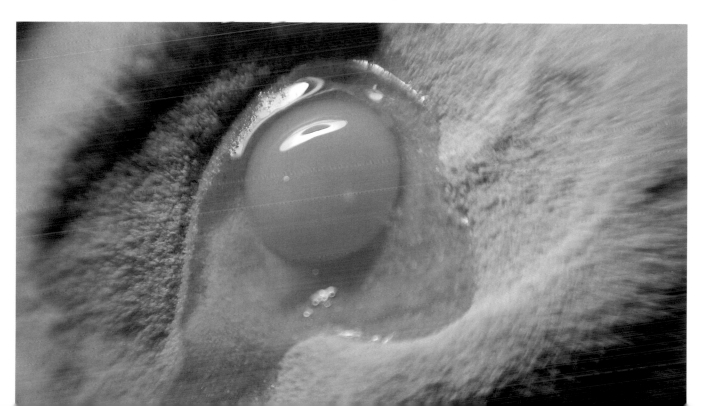

# breakfast

*Hearty country breakfasts begin as soon as the rooster crows, with hot biscuits, sausage, bacon, country ham, gravy, fried eggs, fried apples and fried potatoes. But innkeepers at many of Kentucky's bed-and-breakfast inns serve lighter and more creative fare.*

# glazed bacon

Kentucky's bed-and-breakfast industry is growing rapidly, housed in buildings that range from restored hotels to historic homes.

Todd Allen and Tyler Horton, owners/innkeepers at Maple Hill Manor in Springfield, bought an established bed-and-breakfast when they decided to leave the corporate world and return to their Kentucky roots.

The house, built in 1851 by Thomas McElroy for his bride, Sarah, served as a Confederate hospital during the Battle of Perryville. For a dozen years it was used as a barn, and later it served as a children's home.

One of Maple Hill's breakfast specialties is glazed bacon.

1/2 cup flour

1/3 cup brown sugar

1 teaspoon freshly ground black pepper

1 teaspoon cinnamon, optional

1 pound thick-sliced bacon

Preheat the oven to 300 degrees. Line a cookie sheet with parchment paper to keep the bacon from sticking. Combine the flour, brown sugar, pepper and cinnamon in a gallon-size resealable bag. Place one piece of bacon at a time in the bag. Shake to coat the bacon well. Place the bacon on the cookie sheet so the slices are not touching. Bake for 30 to 40 minutes. Drain on paper towels.

# spanish quiche quesadilla

*Free-range chickens are becoming an important commodity for Kentucky farmers; the eggs are in demand by chefs at upscale restaurants.*

*Some of the best egg recipes come from the Kentucky Egg Council, which sponsors an egg recipe contest each year. The cook-off is held at the Kentucky State Fair. This recipe was the 2004 winner.*

6 jalapeño and herb wraps

1/2 to 1 cup canned black beans

1 cup shoe-peg corn

2 tablespoons finely chopped
   jalapeño pepper

1/2 cup finely chopped green pepper

1 cup reduced-fat Mexican-blend
   cheese

6 eggs

1 teaspoon pepper blend

1 teaspoon ground cumin

1/2 teaspoon chili powder

1/3 cup finely chopped fresh cilantro

14-ounce can diced tomatoes and
   green chilies

1/2 cup milk

Sour cream, optional

Salsa, optional

Preheat the oven to 375 degrees. Coat the bottom and sides of a 9-inch baking dish with olive oil cooking spray. Cover the bottom and sides of the baking dish using 3 wraps. It might be necessary to divide one wrap in half to cover the bottom completely.

Add the ingredients to the baking dish in layers. Pour the black beans and spread evenly onto the wraps. Repeat in the following order: shoe-peg corn, jalapeño peppers, green peppers and cheese.

Whisk the eggs thoroughly in a large mixing bowl. Add the dry spices, cilantro and diced tomatoes and green chilies. Add the milk and blend thoroughly. Pour the blended egg mixture into the baking dish, filling to the top. Bake for 35 minutes and remove the pan from the oven.

Place the 3 remaining wraps on the top. Again, it might be necessary to divide one wrap in half to fully cover the top. Cover the dish with aluminum foil. Return to the oven for 10 minutes or until a knife inserted comes out clean. Quesadilla may be served with the sour cream and salsa. Makes 6 servings.

# snug hollow oatmeal pancakes

*Snug Hollow Farm Bed & Breakfast is tucked away on a 300-acre farm in Red Lick Valley in Estill County. There are no televisions or air conditioning, and nothing to do except rock on the porch, hike, read and eat. Owner/innkeeper Barbara Napier prepares vegetarian meals for her guests, but few notice there's no meat in the house.*

*Napier's recipe for oatmeal pancakes came from a guest who was visiting Kentucky from Scotland. Snug Hollow oatmeal pancakes are a favorite of guests.*

1 cup thick-rolled oats
1 cup all-purpose flour
1/2 cup whole wheat flour
2 1/2 teaspoons baking powder
Pinch of salt
2 large eggs
2 cups milk or buttermilk
5 tablespoons butter, melted
2 tablespoons brown sugar

Combine the oats, flours, baking powder and salt in a large mixing bowl and mix well. Beat the eggs in a separate bowl. Add the buttermilk, butter and brown sugar and mix well. Pour the wet ingredients into dry ingredients and mix well.

Let the mixture sit for 5 minutes. Add a little more milk if the batter is too dry. Heat the griddle. Pour the batter by the half-cup onto the coated griddle. Pancakes are generally ready to flip when they first begin to bubble and stiffen on top. Makes 10 pancakes. Garnish with gingered bananas and serve with warm pure maple syrup.

## GINGERED BANANAS

2 tablespoons butter
1 tablespoon freshly grated ginger
1 banana, peeled and sliced

Melt the butter in a medium skillet. Sprinkle in the ginger. Add the bananas and stir. Let simmer for 1 minute.

# peach-blueberry jam

*Georgia is famous for its peaches, and some Kentuckians will make a trek south early each summer to bring them back to the Bluegrass to sell at farmers markets. But Bath County peaches are making those Georgia peaches blush with shame.*

*The combination of peaches and blueberries in this jam creates a beautiful color.*

3 cups peeled, pitted and finely
   chopped peaches
1/2 cup water
1 pound fresh blueberries
2 tablespoons lemon juice
3 cups sugar

Combine the peaches and water in a large stockpot. Cover and bring just to a boil. Reduce the heat, uncover and simmer, stirring frequently, for about 10 minutes. The peaches will become thick and bubble. Stir in the blueberries; cover and return mixture to a boil. Uncover and simmer for 10 minutes. Add the lemon juice and sugar, 1/2 cup at a time, waiting for the liquid to return to a boil before adding more. Simmer for 5 minutes.

Fill hot sterilized pint jars to within 1/2 inch of lip. Wipe rim clean and attach sterilized lids and screw caps tightly. Process the jars in a boiling water bath for 10 minutes. Makes 6 pints.

# crème brûlée french toast

*Rose and Gary Burke own the Meeting House Bed-and-Breakfast in the heart of Frankfort, Kentucky's capital. The house, circa 1840, is rich in political history.*

*They serve their guests crème brûlée French toast for breakfast.*

1/2 cup unsalted butter

1 cup packed brown sugar

2 teaspoons corn syrup

6 slices French bread, 1 inch thick

5 eggs

1 1/2 cups half-and-half

1 teaspoon vanilla extract

2 teaspoons orange brandy

1/4 teaspoon salt

Melt the butter in a small saucepan over medium heat. Add the brown sugar and corn syrup, stirring until the brown sugar is dissolved. Pour into a 9x13-inch baking dish or individual crème brûlée dishes.

Arrange the bread slices in a single layer in the baking dish. Whisk the eggs, half-and-half, vanilla extract, orange brandy and salt in a small bowl. Pour over the bread and cover. Chill for at least 8 hours or overnight.

Preheat the oven to 350 degrees. Remove the dish from the refrigerator and bring to room temperature. Bake for about 35 minutes or until golden brown. Makes 6 to 8 servings.

# brunch sandwich

*Bed-and-breakfast inns are noted for their overnight casseroles, which make morning meal preparations less stressful. This simple one is from Linda Donovan, innkeeper at Stockton Station Inn in Flemingsburg.*

16 slices bread, buttered, with crusts removed

8 slices sharp Cheddar cheese

8 slices deli ham

6 eggs

3 cups milk

1/2 teaspoon dry mustard

1/2 pound sautéed mushrooms

1 cup crushed cornflakes

1/2 cup melted butter

Place 8 slices of the buttered bread on the bottom of a well-greased 9x13-inch baking dish. Top each slice of the bread with one slice of the cheese and ham. Cover with the remaining 8 slices of bread, buttered side up. Combine the eggs, milk and mustard in a mixing bowl. Pour over the bread. Cover and refrigerate overnight. Remove from the refrigerator. Place the mushrooms on top of the casserole. Sprinkle the top with the cornflakes mixed with melted butter. Bake at 350 degrees for 45 minutes. Makes 8 to 10 servings.

# beverages

*Tea and lemonade are drink choices at luncheons on the porch and at afternoon parties. Kentucky wines and hand-crafted bourbons add life to nighttime parties.*

# mint juleps

Sweet tea, bourbon and mint juleps are traditional Kentucky beverages. There's an art to making all three.

Kentucky has numerous distillers who hand-craft bourbons in small batches, and people who love bourbon will argue about which is best. When it comes to mint juleps, no matter how good the bourbon, it's more about romance than taste.

The julep has become a symbol of the Kentucky Derby and Southern hospitality. Only at Derbytime do Kentucky hosts and hostesses offer their guests mint juleps.

Everyone agrees that the whiskey must be straight-aged Kentucky bourbon, the water must be cold and fresh from a limestone spring, and the julep must be served in a silver cup that is as frosty as a January morning.

But not everyone agrees on how it all comes together.

The formulas, the secrets and descriptions for making juleps are endless. You'll find various accounts in history books as well as cookbooks.

This is one version of the julep.

1/2 cup sugar

1/2 cup water

8 sprigs mint

Crushed ice

3/4 cup to 1 1/2 cups bourbon

Combine the sugar and water in a saucepan. Bring to a boil and stir. Reduce the heat and simmer for 1 to 2 minutes. Pour the syrup into a pint jar. Cover and refrigerate until cold.

For each drink: Measure 1 jigger (1 1/2 ounces or 3 tablespoons) of the syrup into each julep cup or glass. Add 1 sprig of mint to each. Lightly crush the mint using a wooden spoon. Pack each cup with crushed ice. Add 1 to 2 jiggers of the bourbon and stir to mix. Pack to the rim with crushed ice. Garnish each with a mint sprig. Serve at once with straws. Makes 4 drinks.

# sweet tea

On a hot summer day nothing tastes better than a glass of sweet tea.

You don't have to be specific about the ice; sweet tea means iced tea with lots of sugar. There's a fine line between sweet and extra sweet tea, and not everyone can make that perfect pitcher.

"It's an art," said former Herald-Leader reporter Jay Grelen, who now writes a column that he calls "Sweet Tea" for the Arkansas Democrat-Gazette. He has made it his duty to preserve the dignity and sanctity of sweet iced tea.

A lot of Kentuckians feel the same way about sweet tea, but Grelen said it best: "Sweet tea embodies all that is good about the South and its hospitality."

2 quarts water
6 regular-size tea bags
1 regular-size orange spice-flavored
  tea bag
3⁄4 cup sugar

Bring 1 quart of the water just to a boil in a tea kettle. Place the tea bags in a 4-quart container. Pour the hot water over the tea bags and steep for 5 minutes. Place the sugar in a 2-quart pitcher. Add the hot tea and stir until the sugar dissolves. Fill the pitcher with 1 quart of cold water and stir. Serve over ice. Makes 2 quarts.

# a perfect cup of tea

*Bruce and Shelley Richardson, owners of Perryville's Elmwood Inn Fine Teas, Kentucky's only tea blender, have been instrumental in making tea almost as popular in Kentucky as it is in England.*

*Here are the Richardsons' instructions for brewing a perfect cup of tea.*

Filtered water
Loose tea leaves
Milk, lemon or sugar, optional

Fill a good-quality electric or stovetop kettle with cold filtered water and begin heating.

Warm a porcelain teapot with hot but not boiling water. Discard the water in the teapot before putting the tea leaves in the pot.

Place the loose tea leaves - 1 teaspoon dry leaves per cup - in the teapot or use an infuser basket or tea ball and put it in the pot. Pour the hot or boiling water from the kettle over the leaves in the teapot. Agitate the pot occasionally and brew for 4 to 5 minutes.

Remove the infuser basket or tea ball so the tea will not be overbrewed. Use a strainer when pouring the brewed tea into a cup if the tea leaves were put directly in the pot.

Taste the tea before making additions such as milk, lemon or sugar. Milk is generally not added to flavored, green or oolong teas.

Note: Use boiling water only with black or herbal tea. Green, oolong or white tea should use water with a temperature lower than 190 degrees.

# kentucky rosé slush

Kentucky was a major commercial wine-making state more than 200 years ago. Now, after years of dormancy, Kentucky is producing quality wines again.

Central Kentucky is well-suited for growing grapes. One of its award-winning wineries is Springhill Vineyards in Bloomfield, owned by Eddie and Carolyn O'Daniel. The O'Daniels also operate Springhill Plantation Bed & Breakfast. This recipe for a rosé slush is one the O'Daniels serve for Derby parties and summer events.

4 cups water

2 1/2 cups sugar

6-ounce can frozen pineapple juice, thawed

6-ounce can frozen orange juice concentrate, thawed

1/2 cup lemon juice

5 bananas, mashed

1 to 1 1/2 liters ginger ale

750-milliliter bottle Springhill Winery rosé

Bring the water and sugar to a boil in a 2 1/2-quart saucepan. Boil until the sugar dissolves, stirring frequently. Remove the pan from heat and add the pineapple juice, orange juice concentrate, lemon juice and bananas; stir until dissolved. Pour the mixture into 10 ice cube trays or any type of mold and freeze until firm. Transfer the frozen cubes into zippered plastic bags. Store in the freezer until just before serving.

Place the ice cubes or mold in a punch bowl when ready to serve. Add the ginger ale. Ladle into punch cups. The mashed bananas give this a rich and thick flavor that blends nicely with the Springhill rosé. Makes 12 to 15 servings.

# lemonade syrup

*Cooks have placed their faith in Kentucky's cooking bible, What's Cooking in Kentucky by Irene Hayes of Hueysville, for more than three decades.*

*Hayes wrote the book to raise money to "put a roof on our church." She gave all the profits from the book to Hueysville Church of Christ for five years. Not only did the proceeds pay for a new roof but also a Volkswagen bus and new restrooms for the church. The church sold 1,500 books in one month for $2.95 each. Hayes also published What's Cooking for the Holidays, New Year's Through Christmas in 1984. Both books have been reprinted several times and continue to be best sellers.*

*This recipe, from What's Cooking in Kentucky, is for lemonade syrup. When guests drop by, simply add a couple of tablespoons of syrup to a glass of ice water. Add a lemon slice for a great hot-weather cooler.*

2 cups sugar

1 cup water

Pinch of salt

Rind of 2 lemons, cut into small pieces

Juice of 6 lemons

Note: You may use 1 tablespoon syrup and 2 tablespoons orange or pineapple juice. You also may use carbonated water if desired.

Combine the sugar, water, salt and lemon rind in a saucepan. Bring to a boil and boil for 5 minutes. Cool and add the lemon juice. Strain the syrup into a quart jar and store, covered, in the refrigerator. Makes 2 cups syrup or sixteen 8-ounce glasses of lemonade.

Add 2 tablespoons of the syrup to an 8-ounce glass of cold water to serve. Add ice cubes and garnish with a sprig of fresh mint.

# salads & soups

*The best places to shop for produce are farmers markets across the state. Family meals or fanciful dinners often begin with produce picked fresh from a small farm or a back-yard garden.*

# bibb lettuce salad

Traditional Kentucky salad recipes used mostly dandelion greens and wilted lettuce until the late 19th century, when Kentucky salads took on a gourmet flavor.

That was when Jack Bibb first cultivated limestone lettuce. Bibb was in his 80s when he began giving lettuce plants and seeds to friends and neighbors, and it became known as Bibb lettuce. It was produced commercially in 1935.

Bibb was born in 1789 in Virginia and moved with his family to Russellville when he was a boy. He moved to Frankfort in 1845 and built Gray Gables at Wapping Street and Watson Court. His back yard and garden extended to the Kentucky River, and that's where he cultivated the lettuce that bears his name.

This is a recipe that's great for a dinner party.

2 tablespoons melted butter

1/3 cup plus 1 teaspoon brown sugar, divided

3 tablespoons bourbon, divided

2 cups pecan halves

3/4 cup apple cider vinegar

1/2 cup olive oil

2 bunches Bibb lettuce

Crumbled blue or feta cheese

1/2 cup cubed country ham

Preheat the oven to 350 degrees. Combine the melted butter, 1/3 cup brown sugar and 2 tablespoons bourbon in a bowl. Add the pecans and coat. Spread the pecans onto an ungreased cookie sheet and bake for about 10 minutes. Let cool.

Whisk the apple cider vinegar, olive oil, 1 tablespoon bourbon and 1 teaspoon brown sugar in a bowl. Place in refrigerator to chill for at least 30 minutes.

Wash and drain the lettuce. Tear the lettuce into bite-size pieces and place in a serving bowl. Add the crumbled cheese and country ham. Toss with the dressing mixture and sprinkle with the pecans. Serve immediately. Makes 4 servings.

# jonathan's kentucky hot slaw

*Jonathan Lundy, chef/owner of Jonathan at Gratz Park in Lexington, has redefined regional cuisine. His restaurant has what he calls "a Southern backbone with influences from all over."*

*While dining at a restaurant in Northern Kentucky, Lundy was inspired to create Kentucky hot slaw. "They had something similar to this, and I was intrigued by it. I ate it, and it spurred me in a different direction."*

## APPLE CIDER-BACON VINAIGRETTE:

1 cup brown sugar

1/2 teaspoon onion powder

1/2 teaspoon garlic powder

1 tablespoon Dijon mustard

1/2 cup whole-grain prepared mustard

4 tablespoons maple syrup

1 tablespoon Maker's Mark bourbon

1 cup cider vinegar

1 cup rendered bacon fat

1 cup olive oil

To make apple cider-bacon vinaigrette: Combine the brown sugar, onion powder, garlic powder, mustards, syrup, bourbon and vinegar in a mixing bowl; stir. Add the bacon fat and olive oil while whisking slowly. Set aside.

## HOT SLAW:

1 tablespoon vegetable oil

1 cup crispy bacon

6 cups thinly sliced green cabbage

1 1/2 cups julienned carrots

1 cup thinly sliced red onions

3 tablespoons small diced red pepper

1 1/2 cups julienned Granny Smith apples

To make hot slaw: Heat a large sauté pan over high heat. Add the oil and 1/2 the bacon to the pan. Cook for about 1 minute, tossing often. Add the cabbage, carrots, onions, red pepper and apples; sauté for about 1 minute. Deglaze the pan with the vinaigrette. Simmer for about 1 minute. Remove from the heat and place on serving plates. Garnish with more vinaigrette and the remaining crispy bacon. Makes 4 to 6 servings.

# sweet & savory broccoli salad

*Gayle Deaton is a Southern Appalachian cook who, with James Hurm, owns Phoebe's on Main in Beattyville. Gayle made this broccoli salad when she owned a catering business and The Feed Store in Jackson in the '90s.*

DRESSING:

2 cups mayonnaise

3 tablespoons sugar

1 1/2 tablespoons vinegar

SALAD:

12 ounces bacon, fried crisp and crumbled

6 cups broccoli florets

1/2 cup chopped red onion

3/4 cup raisins or dried cranberries

1 1/3 cups salted roasted sunflower kernels

Combine the dressing ingredients in a mixing bowl; set aside. Combine the salad ingredients in a large bowl. Add the dressing and toss to coat. Refrigerate until serving time. Keeps well in a tightly sealed container for a couple of days. Makes 6 to 8 servings.

# warm asparagus spinach salad

*Mason County is considered the "asparagus bed" of Kentucky because of its fertile soil. Every spring the town of May's Lick holds an asparagus festival, and one of the activities is the Taste of Asparagus. Cooks prepare the fresh asparagus dozens of ways, in soup, bread, main dishes and desserts.*

*This spinach salad recipe is from Mason County.*

1 pound fresh asparagus, cut into
    1-inch pieces
2 tablespoons plus 1/2 cup olive oil,
    divided
1/4 teaspoon sea salt
1/2 pound penne pasta
1/2 cup diced onion
6 tablespoons white wine vinegar
2 tablespoons soy sauce
8 ounces fresh baby spinach
3/4 cup cashews
1/2 cup freshly grated Parmesan cheese

Place the asparagus in a 9x13-inch baking
dish and drizzle with the 2 tablespoons
olive oil. Sprinkle with the sea salt. Bake,
uncovered, at 400 degrees for 20 minutes
or until tender. Cook the pasta according
to the package directions and drain.
Combine the onion, vinegar and soy sauce
in a blender. Add the 1/2 cup olive oil
gradually. Combine the spinach, pasta and
asparagus in a serving bowl. Pour the
vinegar mixture over the top and sprinkle
with the cashews and Parmesan cheese.
Serve immediately. Makes 4 to 6 servings.

# orange marmalade dressing

*A.J. Caudill, executive chef at the historic Boone Tavern in Berea, created this orange marmalade dressing for smoked salmon and arugula salad. The recipe is one of his most-requested.*

2 tablespoons chopped white onion

7 tablespoons apple cider vinegar

1 cup orange marmalade

1 cup salad oil (not olive oil)

Purée the onion in a food processor. Add the vinegar and marmalade and purée until smooth. Add the oil slowly while the machine is running. Makes 2 cups.

Serve on smoked salmon and arugula salad.

## SMOKED SALMON AND ARUGULA SALAD:

Toss peppery arugula leaves with the orange marmalade dressing. Top with shavings of white Cheddar cheese, slices of sweet red onions, grape tomatoes, mandarin oranges, toasted almonds and smoked salmon flakes.

# french dressing

*My sister-in-law Margaret Wiseman likes to make salad dressings from scratch. This is one of our family favorites.*

1/3 cup sugar
1/3 cup ketchup
1/3 cup vinegar
1 teaspoon salt
1 cup canola oil
1 clove garlic

Combine the sugar, ketchup, vinegar and salt in a blender. Slowly add the oil with the blender on medium speed. Pour the dressing into a pint jar. Split the clove of garlic and drop it into the dressing. Place the lid on the jar and refrigerate. Shake the jar before serving. Be careful when pouring dressing so the garlic clove remains in the jar. Makes 1 pint.

# green garlic soup

Leo and Jean Pitches Keene own Blue Moon Farm in Madison County, where they grow 28 varieties of gourmet garlic. In the spring the farm sells green garlic, which is used like a scallion; late spring is the time for garlic scapes, the flower stem of a hardneck garlic. Here's the Keenes' recipe for green garlic soup.

1 pound green garlic

2 tablespoons butter

3 small white potatoes

3 cups chicken broth

Salt and pepper to taste

2 to 3 tablespoons white wine vinegar

Cut the garlic into thin rounds using all but the roots and tips of the leaves. Sauté the garlic in the butter, in a saucepan, for about 10 minutes over a low flame.

Wash the potatoes but do not peel them. Cut the potatoes into pieces and add to the sautéed garlic. Add the chicken broth. Cook, covered, for about 30 minutes.

Purée the soup, in small batches in your blender, until it is velvet smooth. Pour the purée into the saucepan, adding more broth if the purée is too thick. Add the salt and pepper and reheat. Add the vinegar when the mixture is hot. Ladle into bowls. Makes 2 servings.

# claude's favorite potato soup

*Until my father retired he didn't do anything in the kitchen except fry an egg or make vegetable soup. He soon mastered the art of frying corn bread, and the grandchildren knew that whenever they dropped by to visit, Grandpa would whip up a batch for a snack.*

*Our family no longer has lacy-edged corn bread, because none of us can make it like Grandpa, who died in 2000. The corn bread was his specialty.*

*He also made a good potato soup from scratch until he discovered this simple recipe. His version didn't include garnishes.*

16 ounces frozen hash brown potatoes

1 cup chopped onion

14 1/2-ounce can ready-to-serve chicken broth

2 cups water

10 3/4-ounce can cream of celery soup, undiluted

10 3/4-ounce can cream of chicken soup, undiluted

2 cups milk

Garlic powder, optional

Red pepper flakes, optional

Garnishes: shredded Cheddar cheese, diced cooked ham or bacon

Combine the potatoes, onion, chicken broth and water in a Dutch oven; bring to a boil. Cover, reduce the heat and simmer for 30 minutes. Stir in the soups and milk; heat thoroughly. Add the garlic powder and red pepper flakes to taste. Ladle the soup into bowls and top with garnishes, if desired. Makes 2 1/2 quarts.

Note: Cream of mushroom soup may be substituted for cream of celery soup.

# soup beans

*Soup beans is a country dish through and through. It has only three ingredients: dried pinto beans, water and some type of pork, such as salt pork or ham hock.*

*Appalachian expert Mark Sohn says a traditional soup bean dinner would include buttermilk, corn bread, slices of sweet onions, stalks of green onions and wilted lettuce. Here's his recipe for soup beans.*

1 pound dried pinto beans, washed and picked over for pebbles

7 cups water

8 ounces salt pork or 2 smoked ham hocks to equal 1 pound

Soak the beans in the water overnight using a glass or porcelain container.

Pour the beans and all of the water in which they soaked into a pot. Add the pork. Simmer, covered, for 6 to 8 hours. Add water as needed to keep the beans covered. The beans hold their shape but will be soft throughout when cooked. Remove the pork and serve it as a side dish.

Thicken the broth by boiling it down and mashing in some cooked beans or purée a cup of beans in a food processor and return the purée to the soup. Makes 10 to 12 servings.

# side dishes

*Kentucky cooks are very creative when it comes to side dishes. A back-yard garden full of tomatoes, squashes, green beans, peppers and potatoes will definitely bring out the creativity in a cook.*

Tradition plays a major role in what we serve alongside the roast turkey, barbecued chicken and grilled steaks. Whatever our parents and grandparents prepared holds a special place in our hearts.

Potluck dinners also have influenced our side choices. A great recipe for broccoli casserole or seven-layer salad is passed around to friends and relatives and often ends up in a church or community cookbook.

Many recipes originate with the farmer who is looking for ways to use a bounty of zucchini or as a way to encourage farmers market customers to buy more eggplant.

# fresh corn pudding

Back-yard gardeners and farmers across Kentucky grow a variety of sweet corn. They jostle verbally about who raises the sweetest variety, and they toss around words like super-sweet, incredible, temptation, precious gem and ambrosia.

As if the corn weren't sweet enough, Kentuckians put it into a dish called corn pudding. It goes great with country ham, fried chicken or beef tenderloin and is on the fanciest luncheon or Kentucky Derby party menus.

This recipe is from well-known Lexington caterer Christine Gilmore and appears in the cookbook *Bluegrass Winners*.

6 to 8 ears of corn

6 whole eggs, stirred well but not beaten

3 cups heavy cream

1/2 cup sugar

1 teaspoon salt

1 teaspoon all-purpose flour

1/2 teaspoon baking powder

2 teaspoons butter, melted

Strip the cobs, barely cutting through the tips of the corn kernels using a sharp paring knife, until you have 3 cups of corn. Scrape the cobs to remove the remaining juice and pulp. Pour the corn into a large mixing bowl and stir in the eggs and cream. Combine the dry ingredients and add to the corn mixture. Stir in the melted butter and mix well. Pour into a greased 2-quart baking dish. Bake at 350 degrees for about 1 hour or until a knife inserted in the center comes out clean. Makes 8 servings.

Note: To make ahead of time, combine the dry ingredients in a jar and wet ingredients in another jar. Combine the two just before cooking.

# louise's corn pudding

*Louise Thompson, my mother-in-law, found a simpler way to make corn pudding. This is a dish she always made at the last minute when she decided she didn't have enough side dishes for the holiday dinner.*

16-ounce can whole kernel corn, drained

3 tablespoons all-purpose flour

Salt and pepper

1/4 cup sugar

1 egg, beaten

3 tablespoons butter, melted

Milk

Combine all of the ingredients, except the milk, in a 2-quart microwaveable dish. Add enough milk to cover. Microwave on high, uncovered, for 10 minutes. Stir as the mixture cooks. Makes 6 to 8 servings.

# tomato gravy

*Some of the best cooks in Kentucky have invited me into their homes to talk about cooking and recipes. Some leave a lasting impression, even years later. One of those cooks was the late Margaret Blakemore of Winchester. She was a collector of iron skillets, and I interviewed her in 1989.*

*Mrs. Blakemore was raised in Louisiana and used her iron cookware to prepare Cajun dishes, including tomato gravy.*

4 slices bacon

2 tablespoons all-purpose flour

1 medium onion, chopped

14 1/2-ounce can diced tomatoes

Water

Cooked rice

Fry the bacon in a skillet until crisp. Remove bacon and save for another use. Pour off all but about 2 tablespoons of the grease. Add the flour. Cook for several minutes over low heat, stirring constantly with a wooden spoon, until the mixture, known as a roux, is medium brown. Add the onion, tomatoes and a tomato can of water to the roux and stir. Simmer until thick. Serve over the cooked rice. Makes 4 servings.

# tomato and chipotle salsa

*Lexington chef John Foster practices the philosophy that food grown locally tastes better than food shipped in from elsewhere. He has planned his daily restaurant menus depending on what was fresh and available from Central Kentucky farmers. During the summer he makes this salsa.*

8 tomatoes, peeled and chopped

2 red bell peppers, chopped

2 green bell peppers, chopped

1 yellow onion, chopped

2 ounces fresh cilantro, chopped

3 chipotle chilies, chopped

Juice of 4 limes

Juice of 1 lemon

1 teaspoon cumin

1 teaspoon red chili powder

1 tablespoon chopped garlic

2 tablespoons olive oil

Salt to taste

Combine the tomatoes, bell peppers and onion in a large bowl and mix well. Add the cilantro, chipotle chilies, lime juice, lemon juice, cumin, chili powder, garlic and olive oil; mix well. Season with the salt. Chill, covered, until ready to serve. Serve with chips or quesadillas. Makes 12 servings.

# roasted asparagus

*Asparagus is one of the first crops harvested in spring. Roasting is one of the tastiest ways to cook fresh asparagus, which is best when the stalks are thin.*

2 pounds asparagus, tough ends
   trimmed
1/4 cup olive oil
Sea salt
Freshly ground garlic-pepper
   seasoning

Preheat the oven to 400 degrees. Toss the asparagus with the olive oil, salt and seasoning. Spread the asparagus on a baking sheet. Roast for 15 minutes or until the asparagus is tender and begins to brown. Serve hot or warm. Makes 6 servings.

# roasted vegetables

*Kentucky's growing season is from late April to early November. Farmers raise everything from green onions to gourmet mushrooms. Roasting is a great way to cook vegetables after a trip to the roadside stand or farmers market.*

1 small eggplant (about 1 pound), cut into 3/4-inch pieces

1 medium zucchini, cut into 3/4-inch pieces

1 small green bell pepper, cut into 3/4-inch pieces

1 large portobello mushroom, cut into 3/4-inch pieces

1 1/2 cups cherry tomatoes, halved

4 green onions, thinly sliced

1 to 2 tablespoons olive oil

1 tablespoon balsamic vinegar

1 clove garlic, minced

2 teaspoons dried basil leaves

Sea salt and freshly ground black pepper to taste

Preheat the oven to 450 degrees. Combine all of the ingredients in a large bowl. Spread in a shallow 9x13-inch casserole dish. Cover loosely with aluminum foil and bake for 10 minutes. Remove the foil and bake for 35 to 45 minutes or until the vegetables are soft and any liquid in the bottom of the casserole dish has evaporated. Cool before serving. Makes 4 to 6 servings.

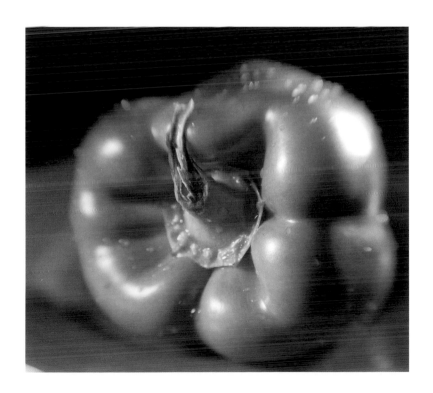

# elizabeth witt's summer squash

*In the early 1950s, Harry and Elizabeth Witt of Irvine began buying toys for children and delivering them at Christmastime. It was something they did for more than 20 years. In 1975, when Harry Witt died, his widow decided to have children come to her house after Irvine's annual Christmas parade and she continued the tradition until her death in 1990.*

*Elizabeth Witt was also known as an outstanding cook; she shared this recipe with us when she was 85. "I was visiting (friends) at their home on Lake Cumberland, and before I left she served my companion and me a lunch plate, and when she asked if we liked squash, I asked her to give me a very small portion as I was not too fond of squash," Mrs. Witt said. "And to her delight and surprise, I passed my plate for a second helping."*

3 cups zucchini, cubed

3 cups early summer squash, cubed

1/4 cup onion, diced

10 3/4-ounce can cream of chicken soup

1 cup sour cream

1 cup shredded carrots

6-ounce package corn bread-flavored
  stuffing mix

Butter

Paprika

Place the zucchini, squash and onion in a saucepan. Add water to cover and bring to a boil. Cover and boil for 5 minutes; drain. Combine the soup, sour cream, carrots and the package of herbs from the stuffing mix in a mixing bowl. Add the soup mixture to the drained squash. Lightly butter a 9x13-inch baking dish. Place 1/2 of the corn bread stuffing on the bottom. Spoon in the squash mixture and sprinkle the remaining stuffing on top. Dot with the butter and lightly sprinkle with the paprika. Bake at 350 degrees for 30 minutes. Makes 6 to 8 servings.

# garlic cheese grits

*Grits are as much a part of the South as a Southern drawl.*

*Plain grits are known as "Southern oatmeal," but when cheese and garlic are added, they become Derby fare served in a silver dish.*

6 cups water

2 teaspoons salt

1 1/2 cups grits

1 stick butter

3 eggs, well-beaten

4 cups grated sharp Cheddar cheese

1 to 2 garlic cloves, crushed

Cayenne pepper to taste

Bring the water and salt to a rapid boil in a saucepan. Stir in the grits using a whisk. Cook until all the water is absorbed, stirring occasionally. Stir in the butter. Add the eggs, cheese, garlic and cayenne pepper. Pour into a greased 2 1/2-quart casserole dish. Bake at 350 degrees for 45 minutes to 1 hour or until the top is lightly browned. Makes 8 servings.

# peach butter

*Ouita Michel, chef/owner of Holly Hill Inn in Midway, serves many peach dishes during the summer. "Invariably, we have some (peaches) that are too bruised or have spots or were cut the day before and are beginning to get mushy and turn brown," she said. "I always cook these down in their own juices for a peach butter. The same process works great for carrots and onions. The combinations are endless — this is a great alternative to real butter."*

4 cups peaches, peeled and cut
  into pieces
1/2 cup Riesling or any dry
  white wine

Combine the peaches and wine in a heavy-bottomed pot. Cook over low heat for about 4 hours or until very thick. Add a pinch of sugar or salt, if necessary. Purée in a blender or food processor. Cool and serve on muffins or toast, on ham, chicken salad or olive nut sandwiches.

# entrées

*From the mountains in the east to the flatlands of the west, Kentucky farmers are raising pork, lamb, beef, buffalo, goat, poultry, shrimp and tilapia.*

Kentucky's mild weather allows outdoor cooking practically year-round. Cattlemen are raising high-quality beef that can be placed on the grill without a marinade or rub for added flavor.

We're finding new recipes for seafood because it's being raised within minutes of our homes. We look to lamb producers for their best recipes and to professional chefs for great pork recipes.

Those who cure country hams share their tricks for preserving a heritage food, and regional cookbooks are the best places to find recipes that use it.

Kentucky is known for burgoo. While family recipes abound, few people cook the stew that's practically a day's work.

Western Kentucky is famous for its pork barbecue, slow-cooked over wood and doused with a vinegar-based sauce. Other parts of the state use a variety of sauces but the meat of choice is usually pork, cooked slow using low heat and lots of smoke.

Other dishes we've chosen for this section are ones that have made regional cooks and caterers famous.

# miss patsy's fried chicken

The foods my family ate when I was growing up were fresh and mostly homegrown. There was a hen house in the back yard where we gathered large brown eggs. When company was coming, that's where dinner came from, too.

Sometimes, we had fried chicken in the middle of the week, but my younger brother, Gary Wiseman, and I filled up on the mashed potatoes and green beans because we were not going to eat the chicken no matter how hungry we were. Watching Mom kill the chicken and pluck the feathers was enough to dull our appetites for chicken for decades. It never bothered our older brother, Lynn, because he was off playing softball or fishing in the creek until it was time to eat.

It's difficult to imagine that 50 years ago, planning a fried chicken dinner included going to the yard and catching a young hen. Frying chicken today is a lot easier, but few people make fried chicken at home.

The best Kentucky fried chicken has two truths:

One: The pan-fried kind tastes better than the deep-fried kind.

Two: The best cooking vessel is a blackened cast-iron skillet.

After technique and choice of pan, there is room for debate about how best to make fried chicken. Some cooks like to soak the chicken in milk or buttermilk. Some use a relatively sturdy breading. Others say seasoned flour is the only coating needed.

One of Central Kentucky's most famous cooks was Patsy Bergeon of Paris, who was known for her fried chicken. Miss Patsy, who lived to the age of 82, cooked for Stoner Creek Country Club and Iron Rail Restaurant in Paris.

She guarded her secret for years. But when she became ill, she decided to share it. "I can't take it with me," she told Charles Ramey, whom she taught to fry chicken like she did.

1 whole frying chicken

Vinegar

Salt

2 cups self-rising flour

1 teaspoon garlic powder

1 teaspoon black pepper

2 teaspoons salt

Vegetable shortening

Cut up the chicken. Place the pieces in a pot and sprinkle with the vinegar and salt. Cover with lukewarm water; let stand for about 30 minutes and drain. Combine the flour, 2 tablespoons salt, garlic powder and pepper in a shallow dish. Melt enough vegetable shortening in an iron skillet for about 1 inch of grease.

Dredge the chicken in the flour mixture, shaking off excess flour. Place the chicken into the hot grease. As it cooks, "tickle" the chicken by moving it around gently with tongs. If you have enough grease you won't have to turn it. Listen to the chicken. "When it gets quiet, it's ready to come up," according to Miss Patsy. After about 20 minutes, when chicken pieces are golden brown, lift them from the grease and drain on racks.

# don edwards' chili

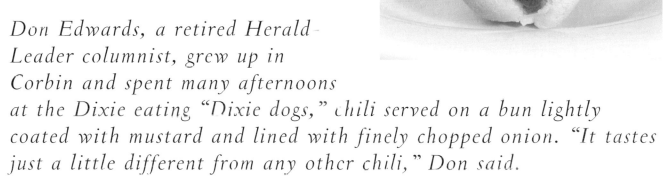

*Almost every small town has had a drive-in or café that served a secret-recipe chili. Corbin had The Dixie Café on Main Street, which closed in August 2005.*

*Don Edwards, a retired Herald-Leader columnist, grew up in Corbin and spent many afternoons at the Dixie eating "Dixie dogs," chili served on a bun lightly coated with mustard and lined with finely chopped onion. "It tastes just a little different from any other chili," Don said.*

*Many legends surround Dixie chili, but the recipe that's closest to the original is this one, even though the Dixie owners claimed the chili did not contain beer. Corbin was dry.*

*An aunt gave this recipe to Don. She had requested it for a former Corbin resident who had moved to California and wanted to taste Dixie chili again. This is Edwards' version of Dixie-style chili.*

3 pounds lean ground beef

12-ounce can or bottle beer

3 teaspoons salt

10-ounce can tomato purée

6 teaspoons chili powder

1 cup crushed corn flakes
  (equivalent of 2 cups not crushed)

Combine the ground beef, beer and salt in a skillet and simmer for 40 minutes. Add the tomato purée, chili powder and crushed corn flakes. Cook an additional 20 minutes. Serve on hot dog buns with mustard and onion or over hot dogs.

# roasted pork tenderloin

*Western Kentucky has a number of pork producers, and many top chefs in the state are choosing to serve locally produced pork on their menus. This recipe for roasted pork tenderloin is from Joe Castro, executive chef at The Brown Hotel in Louisville.*

1 cup dry corn bread crumbs

2 cloves garlic, minced

1 shallot, minced

1 teaspoon minced rosemary

1 teaspoon minced thyme

2 tablespoons olive oil

Salt and pepper to taste

Two 1- to 2- pound pork tenderloins

2 tablespoons Dijon mustard

1/2 cup small diced country ham

1 large sweet onion,
   cut in 1/2-inch pieces

1 tablespoon bourbon

2 cups chicken stock

3 tablespoons unsalted butter

Combine the corn bread crumbs, garlic, shallot, rosemary, thyme and 1 tablespoon of the olive oil in a small bowl. Season the mixture with the salt and pepper.

Season the pork loins with the salt and pepper. Heat the remaining olive oil in an ovenproof skillet over medium-high heat. Gently lay the pork in the skillet when the oil is hot. Sear all sides of the tenderloins until brown.

Remove the skillet from the heat and allow the meat to cool. Spread a thin layer of mustard over the pork. Coat the pork loins with the corn bread mixture. Place the skillet in the oven and cook at 350 degrees for 20 to 30 minutes per pound. Remove the pork from the skillet and keep warm.

Return the skillet to the range and add the country ham and onion. Cook until the onion is golden to dark brown. Deglaze the skillet with the bourbon and add the chicken stock. Reduce the mixture to a sauce consistency and fold in the butter. Adjust the seasoning with the salt and pepper. Pour the sauce over the pork. Makes 6 to 8 servings.

# blue cheese bison burgers

*By the late 1800s, bison were practically extinct. With the combined efforts of ranchers and conservationists, bison are roaming again in Kentucky. We can enjoy bison burgers, steaks and roasts at restaurants and at home. Bison meat, which is low in cholesterol and fat, makes a great burger.*

1 pound ground bison

1 1/2 tablespoons Dijon mustard

1 tablespoon roasted garlic

2 green onions, chopped

1 teaspoon Worcestershire sauce

Salt and pepper to taste

1 or 2 ounces blue cheese

Combine the bison, mustard, garlic, onions, Worcestershire sauce, salt and pepper. Shape into 4 patties, with about 1 teaspoon of blue cheese in the center of each patty. Grill to preferred doneness. Makes 4 servings.

# lamb shanks

*Home cooks usually prepare lamb on special occasions. Kentucky has 1,800 sheep producers, and the number is increasing.*

*Anne and Steve Muntz of Mount Sterling have been farming on a small scale for about 20 years. They raise sheep, chickens, turkeys and an organic garden. Anne created this recipe for lamb shanks.*

2 medium lamb shanks

Olive oil

2 tablespoons beef bouillon

1 large onion

2 tablespoons chopped garlic

2 to 3 large portobello mushrooms, sliced

3 to 4 rosemary sprigs, 1/2-inch long

Salt and pepper to taste

Brown the lamb shanks in the enough olive oil to coat the bottom of a heavy skillet. Add the remaining ingredients, making sure the bouillon is on the bottom. Pour 1 cup of water over all, cover and simmer until the meat is tender and pulls away from the bones. Check frequently to make sure the water hasn't simmered away, adding water as needed to make gravy. Serve over wild or white rice. Makes 4 to 6 servings.

# proctor pie

*Dr. James Hurm is a family practitioner in Beattyville and co-owner of the restaurant Phoebe's on Main.*

*This hearty meat pie, named for the road where Hurm lives, is a combination of two recipes. He recommends using a homemade pie crust for this dish.*

**MEAT PORTION:**

2 tablespoons olive or vegetable oil

1 large onion, chopped

1 clove garlic, peeled and finely chopped

1 pound ground sirloin

1 pound ground pork tenderloin (ask meat cutter to trim off all fat and grind only the lean part)

1 tablespoon allspice

1 teaspoon cinnamon

1/4 teaspoon ground cloves

1 teaspoon salt

8 to 10 grinds black pepper

1/2 cup cracker crumbs

**POTATO TOPPING:**

3 cups cooked, mashed potatoes

3/4 cup half-and-half

1 1/2 tablespoons butter

1 1/4 cups cottage cheese

3/4 cup sour cream

3 eggs

1 teaspoon salt

6 to 8 grinds black pepper

2 1/2 cups grated Cheddar cheese

3/4 cup finely chopped sweet onion

2 unbaked deep-dish 9-inch pie shells (or make your own)

To make meat portion: Add the oil and onion to a heated skillet and sauté until the onion is almost transparent. Add the garlic and sauté for 30 seconds. Remove from the heat and set aside. Brown the meats; strain in a colander and rinse with hot water. Combine the meat, onion-garlic mixture and spices in the skillet. Add enough water to almost cover. Simmer, covered, for 30 minutes. Drain, reserving the liquid. Add the cracker crumbs and just enough of the reserved liquid to make it moist and set aside.

To make potato topping: Combine the potatoes, half-and-half and butter in a bowl. Blend well and set aside. Combine the cottage cheese, sour cream, eggs, salt and pepper in a separate bowl. Beat until smooth using an electric mixer on high speed. Add the potato mixture and beat for 1 minute. Stir in the cheese and onion.

To assemble pie: Divide the meat mixture between the two pie shells. Cover with the potato topping. Bake at 425 degrees for 35 to 40 minutes or until golden brown. Makes 12 to 16 servings.

This dish reheats nicely. It can be made in advance and frozen, unbaked, until ready to use.

# the original hot brown

*Out-of-state visitors can't leave Kentucky without sampling a hot Brown. It's a Kentucky tradition covered in cream sauce. The hot Brown, almost 1,000 calories of piping hot history, was created on a whim by a chef at Louisville's famed Brown Hotel during the Roaring '20s.*

*According to legend, the grand dining room in the Brown Hotel drew more than 1,200 guests each evening for its dinner dance.*

*The band would play into the wee hours, and hungry guests would retire to the restaurant for a midnight snack. The story goes that the cooks grew tired of preparing ham and eggs, so chef Fred Schmidt created an open-faced turkey sandwich with Mornay sauce. At the time turkey was prepared almost exclusively at Thanksgiving and Christmas so this was a treat. The sandwich was broiled with two strips of bacon and some pimento added for color.*

1/2 cup butter

1/2 cup flour

3 to 3 1/2 cups milk

6 tablespoons grated Parmesan cheese

1 egg, beaten

1 ounce heavy whipping cream, optional

Salt and pepper to taste

8 to 12 slices toast, may be trimmed

Slices of roast turkey

Grated Parmesan cheese

8 to 12 strips fried bacon

Melt the butter in a saucepan. Add the flour to make a reasonably thick roux, or paste, that absorbs all the butter. Add the milk and 6 tablespoons Parmesan cheese, stirring constantly. Add the egg to thicken and continue stirring. Do not allow sauce to boil. Remove from the heat. Fold in the cream. Add the salt and pepper.

Place two slices of the toast on a metal or flameproof dish for each hot Brown. Cover the toast with a liberal amount of the turkey. Pour a generous amount of the sauce over the turkey and toast. Sprinkle with the Parmesan cheese. Place the entire dish under a broiler until the sauce is speckled brown and bubbly. Remove from the broiler and place two pieces of the bacon crosswise on top. Serve immediately. Makes 4 hot Browns.

# kentucky burgoo

*Visitors to Kentucky want to try dishes that are rarely found outside the state's borders. One of our legendary offerings is burgoo, a Kentucky stew that originally was made with any wild game on hand.*

*Burgoo has been served at Keeneland Race Course since it opened in 1936, and today is one of the most popular items on the menu.*

*When out-of-state racing fans ask what's in burgoo, native Kentuckians will sometimes tell them rabbit, squirrel, pheasant, grouse, venison, quail and a few vegetables. Today's version features pork and beef instead of the game and fowl that were once popular.*

*Keeneland's burgoo recipe is virtually the same as it was in 1936, except for the type of meat used. Here's a recipe from Turf Catering, which runs Keeneland's concessions, for Kentucky burgoo.*

Oil

3 pounds stew meat, cubed

1 teaspoon ground thyme

1 teaspoon sage

1 teaspoon oregano

1 teaspoon minced garlic

1 cup diced celery

1 cup diced carrot

1 cup diced onion

12-ounce can diced tomatoes in juice

Two 16-ounce cans mixed vegetables

7-ounce can tomato purée

2 pounds sliced fresh okra

1 tablespoon beef base

1 teaspoon Worcestershire sauce

1 cup sherry

3 pounds potatoes, peeled and diced

Cornstarch

Heat the oil in a large Dutch oven. Brown the stew meat with the herbs and garlic. Add the remaining ingredients, except cornstarch, and cover with water. Bring to a boil, reduce heat and simmer for at least 3 hours. Adjust seasonings to taste and thicken with the cornstarch. Makes 10 to 12 servings.

# barbecued ribs

*Rory Snowden, owner of Tobago Ribs in Lexington, uses a rich sweet sauce to glaze pork ribs that he smokes over a charcoal fire. Most pit masters have a secret sauce. Here are instructions on how to smoke baby back ribs, which are more tender than spareribs.*

4 full racks pork baby back ribs
Liquid marinade of choice
Dry rub of choice
4 cups barbecue sauce of choice

Peel the membrane from the underside of the ribs using a paring knife and your fingers; discard the membrane. Place the ribs in a large resealable bag or in a large disposable aluminum pan. Pour the marinade over the ribs. Seal or cover and refrigerate for at least 4 hours. Remove the ribs from the marinade but do not pat dry. Discard the marinade.

Place the ribs on a baking sheet and sprinkle with the dry rub, coating evenly. Let the ribs stand at room temperature for about 15 minutes or until the surface of the ribs is tacky.

Prepare a fire in a smoker. Place the ribs directly on the smoker rack, add wood chips to the coals and close the lid. Smoke at 225 to 250 degrees for 2 1/2 hours. Brush ribs with barbecue sauce, close lid and smoke for 30 to 60 minutes or until meat pulls away from the ends of the bones. Makes 4 servings.

# curried kentucky goat

*More Kentucky farmers, especially in Western Kentucky, are raising goats.*

*Kevin Toyoda, executive chef at Bella Notte restaurant in Lexington, said he cooks goat two ways: braised with a homemade Jamaican style curry; and roasted whole on a spit for about 6 hours. "The best way was braised," he said.*

SPICE RUB:

1 cup jerk seasoning

1 cup curry powder

1/2 cup dark brown sugar

2 tablespoons sorghum molasses

3 tablespoons kosher salt

1 1/2 tablespoons cracked
   black pepper

1/2 cup olive oil

3 to 4 pound goat shoulder or hind quarter, bone-in

2 pounds carrots

2 pounds onions

2 garlic bulbs

6 ounces tomato paste

1/4 cup olive oil

2 cups red wine

1 pound hot curry paste dissolved in 1 quart
   warm water

Water to cover

Preheat oven to 400 degrees. Combine all of the ingredients for spice rub and set aside. Rinse the meat under cold water and dry with a paper towel. Rub the meat aggressively with the spice paste and let the meat set for 30 minutes, allowing the internal temperature of the meat to stabilize for best cooking results.

Peel and dice the carrots and onions into about 1 inch squares. Crush the garlic with the heel of your hand. Toss the carrots, onion, garlic, tomato paste and olive oil in a roasting pan deep enough to contain the roast and the liquid. Roast the vegetables in the oven, stirring every 6 to 7 minutes, until they are lightly caramelized.

Remove the pan from the oven and deglaze it with the red wine, being sure to scrape everything from the bottom of the pan. Turn the oven temperature to 325 degrees.

Sear the meat on a very hot, preferably wood-burning, grill. The meat will char and lightly blacken to form a rich caramelized crust. Transfer the meat, when it is completely seared, to the pan with the roasted vegetables. Add any remaining spice rub and the dissolved curry paste. Cover the meat and vegetables completely with hot water and weigh down the meat with a heavy, oven-safe plate. Cover the pan with aluminum foil to form a tight seal, leaving a small corner open for a steam vent. Place the pan on the stove over a medium-high heat, allowing the liquid to come to a boil.

Transfer the pan to the oven when steam begins to escape through the vent, letting the meat cook undisturbed for 3 hours. Remove the pan from the oven and carefully remove the aluminum foil. The meat should fall from the bone with a little prodding from a fork; if not, reseal the pan and place it back in the oven until the desired results are achieved. Allow the meat to cool in the juices for 30 to 40 minutes to ensure maximum flavor. Serve with cannellini or black beans, steamed rice and mango salsa.

# mcdowell farms meatloaf

*Belinda Fay and Carla McDowell are known in Kentucky as the "Salsa Sisters." They produce McDowell Farms Salsa in Germantown in Mason County.*

*They started the business as a tribute to their mother, Doris McCormick, who died in the summer of 2002, when the family gardens were at their peak.*

*"We chopped and cooked and cried. It was our way to get through the summer and get Dad (Carl McCormick) through it. It was our definition of going through the grieving process," Carla said.*

*Belinda and Carla developed this recipe for meatloaf using their salsa as a flavorful ingredient.*

3 pounds ground chuck

2 eggs

3/4 cup cracker crumbs or oats

8-ounce jar McDowell Farms salsa

1/2 cup ketchup

Salt and pepper to taste

Combine all of the ingredients in a large bowl and mix well. Place the mixture in a loaf pan. Cover with additional ketchup, as desired. Bake at 350 degrees for 1 hour.

# eggplant parmesan

*Jimmy Thompson of Bath County planted a small plot of eggplant a few years ago. Many of his neighbors didn't know how to cook the fat, purple vegetable, so he handed out recipes for eggplant parmesan at the farmers market. Now he sells every eggplant he grows.*

2 pounds eggplant

1 cup all-purpose flour

Salt and freshly ground black pepper

2 large eggs

1/2 cup water

3 cups dried bread crumbs

Vegetable and olive oil

SAUCE:

1 clove garlic, minced

3 tablespoons olive oil

1 1/2 pounds diced tomatoes

Salt to taste

3/4 cup freshly grated
   Parmesan cheese

Grated Mozzarella cheese

Slice the eggplant into 1/2-inch thick round slices. Place the flour in a bowl and season it with the salt and pepper. Combine the eggs and water in a bowl and beat until frothy. Pour the bread crumbs onto a plate. Dredge the slices in the flour, shaking off the excess. Drop the slices into the eggs. Lay the slices in the crumbs, coating well and pressing the crumbs onto both sides.

Heat a skillet over medium-high heat for 1 or 2 minutes. Pour in about 1/3 inch of the oil. Place the eggplant slices in the hot oil, not overlapping. Brown until golden on both sides and drain on paper towels.

Place the garlic and 3 tablespoons olive oil in a saucepan over a medium heat. Add the tomatoes and salt. Simmer for about 15 minutes. Spoon about 1 cup of the tomato sauce into the bottom of an oiled 8x10-inch casserole dish. Lay about 1/3 of the fried eggplant in the casserole dish. Top with 1/3 of the remaining tomato sauce and 1/4 cup of the Parmesan cheese. Repeat twice. Top with the Mozzarella cheese. Bake at 350 degrees for 30 to 40 minutes. Let it set for 10 minutes before serving. Makes 4 to 6 servings

# grilled tilapia

*Tons of shrimp, catfish, trout, tilapia and spoonfish are being raised in farm ponds all over the state. The seafood is sold pondside to home cooks, caterers and restaurateurs, and some of it goes to Shuckman's Fish Co. & Smokery in Louisville, where it is marinated, cured and smoked.*

*Kentucky is becoming known around the world for its spoonfish caviar, or fish eggs. The spoonfish is native to Kentucky and is a member of the sturgeon family. Kentucky spoonfish caviar is affordable and, unlike some caviar, doesn't have a real fishy or real salty taste.*

*Kentucky's first pond-raised shrimp were harvested in Bourbon County in 1996, and Joe McCord of Clark County was there. He came home and told his wife, Shiela, that if other farmers could raise shrimp in Kentucky, he could, too. They turned a greenhouse, once used to start tobacco plants, into a shrimp nursery and now have six ponds where they raise shrimp and tilapia.*

*Here is Shiela McCord's recipe for grilled tilapia.*

4 tilapia fillets
Butter
Coarse salt
Freshly grated black pepper
Nature's Seasoning

Prepare a medium-hot fire in the grill. Rinse the tilapia, pat it dry. Rub the fish with the butter, salt, pepper and seasoning. Place the fillets in a fish basket and grill for about 3 minutes per side. Makes 4 servings.

# shrimp samuels

*Fresh Kentucky prawns are perfect for this recipe from Bill Samuels Jr., president of Maker's Mark Distillery. This recipe appears in Sandra Davis' That Special Touch cookbook. Davis, who lives in Springfield, wrote it in 1990, and it's still one of Kentucky's most treasured cookbooks. This is a dish that has been scrved at the distillery's Derby Week party.*

3 sticks butter

1/4 pound brown sugar

2 tablespoons fresh thyme

1 tablespoon fresh rosemary

1/2 teaspoon Tabasco sauce

1 tablespoon Worcestershire sauce

1 tablespoon minced garlic

24 large shrimp, peeled

1 tablespoon fresh lemon juice

Salt and pepper to taste

1/4 teaspoon cayenne pepper

4 ounces Maker's Mark

Melt the butter in a large skillet. Add the brown sugar, thyme, rosemary, Tabasco sauce, Worcestershire sauce and garlic and sauté for 2 minutes.

Add the shrimp and cook for about 3 minutes or until pink. Add the remaining ingredients and flame, if desired. Simmer for 2 minutes. Makes 6 servings.

Note: Allow 3/4 to 1 pound per person when buying unpeelcd shrimp to serve as a main dish.

# fried fish

*Western Kentucky, with its immense lakes, is home to many great anglers. After a day on the water, the easiest way to prepare the fresh catch is to fry it and serve it right from the skillet.*

1/2 cup flour, per 3 to 4 fillets
1 cup cornmeal, per 3 to 4 fillets
Salt to taste
Black pepper to taste
Cayenne pepper to taste
Fresh fish, cleaned and filleted
Vegetable oil

Place the flour and cornmeal in a large resealable plastic bag; the amount depends on the number of fish fillets. Add the salt, black pepper and cayenne pepper and shake. Place the fish in the bag and shake until the fish are fully coated. Take the fish fillets from the bag, one at a time, allowing the excess coating to fall back into the bag. Set the fish aside.

Pour about 1 inch of the vegetable oil into a large iron skillet over medium heat. Add the fish to the hot oil and fry for several minutes on each side or until lightly browned. Serve with hush puppies, fried potatoes and coleslaw. The number of servings depends on the size of the catch.

# desserts

*Kentuckians like their sweets. Hand-made candies, luscious cakes and bourbon-laced pies are some of our favorites.*

# jam cake

Growing up in rural Clark County, the chore I hated the most was picking blackberries. Every summer for six years, as soon as the berries were ripe, we picked buckets and buckets of them.

I still remember putting on baggy old pants and a long-sleeve shirt, so the briers wouldn't scratch my arms, and hanging a bucket on my belt. Off we'd go to the patch - my mother, my two brothers and several neighbors. It was an event. We packed lunch and took ice water in a Mason jar.

We would walk what seemed like miles from our house, down the railroad track, to a valley and then up the hillside to the blackberry patch. No one was allowed to go home until all the huge water buckets were filled.

Those days were drudgery. It was hot; June bugs and yellow and black garden spiders were everywhere. I would cry. I came home with chigger bites. I hated blackberries. I hated blackberry jam.

When I was 12 we left Clark County and that dreadful blackberry patch. We moved to Fayette County, where across the country road from our house was a wild blackberry patch. For 25 years, my father picked blackberries and Mom made jam. Each summer Dad would say, "Oh, those berries are the biggest I've ever seen. Come pick with me." And for 25 years I made excuses.

One day he said to me, "I went blackberry picking today. Those are the biggest blackberries I've ever seen." They must be gigantic, I thought, given that they've been growing bigger every year.

I had to see for myself, so I decided to walk over to the patch. It would be wonderful, I figured, to have fresh jam to give friends at Christmastime.

Off I went, a bucket tied onto a belt around my waist. I picked a few berries around the edges of the patch; the more I picked the more I enjoyed it. A brier snagged my arm, but I kept going deeper and deeper into the patch.

My bucket was filled with beautiful, juicy berries in just a matter of minutes. My feelings about berries and briers had definitely changed.

I was delighted with the bucket of berries I had picked. So with berry-stained hands and clothes, and muddy shoes, I ran to a grocery store to buy canning jars, sugar and Sure-Jell.

As I capped those lovely jars of jam, I was very proud of having "discovered" something as wonderfully fresh and delicious as the blackberry.

The next evening I said to my 8-year-old daughter Sarah, "Come pick blackberries with me. They're the biggest I've ever seen."

I put a baggy shirt and pants on her, and tied a bucket to an old belt and buckled it around her tiny waist. Off we went to the blackberry patch.

But somehow, buzzing June bugs, prickly bushes and blackberry juice on her hands did not appeal to Sarah.

I smiled and took her home.

Sarah is now 27 years old, and she makes blackberry jam just like her grandmother did. A couple of rows of thornless blackberry bushes are planted just steps from her kitchen door. Last summer she was delighted to make blackberry jam and proudly give it away at Christmastime saying, "I made it myself."

My mom always saved homemade blackberry jam to use in her jam cakes. Here's the recipe she used.

## JAM CAKE

1 cup butter

2 cups sugar

3 egg yolks

2 eggs

1 cup blackberry jam

1 teaspoon baking soda

3 cups all purpose flour

1 teaspoon nutmeg

1 teaspoon cloves

2 teaspoons cinnamon

1 teaspoon allspice

1 cup buttermilk

1 cup chopped pecans

Icing

Preheat the oven to 350 degrees. Cream the butter and sugar in a large mixing bowl. Beat the egg yolks and eggs in a separate bowl; stir into the creamed mixture. Add the jam. Sift the baking soda, flour and spices in a separate bowl. Add to the creamed mixture, alternately, with the buttermilk. Add the pecans.

Pour into greased and floured cake pans lined with waxed paper. Bake for about 30 minutes or until the cake springs back when touched.

## ICING

1/2 cup melted butter

1 cup brown sugar

1/4 cup milk

1 3/4 to 2 cups powdered sugar

Combine the melted butter and brown sugar in a saucepan. Boil over a low heat for 2 minutes. Stir in the milk and bring to a boil. Remove from the heat and cool. Add the powdered sugar and beat well. Spread between the layers and on the top and sides of the jam cake.

## BLACKBERRY JAM

2 cups fresh blackberries

2 cups sugar

Combine the blackberries and sugar in a large saucepan. Cook over low heat for about 1 hour or until the mixture thickens. It doesn't have to be too thick.

# myrtle's fried apple pies

*In the late 1950s the Willing Workers at Franklin Avenue Church of God in Winchester made fried apple pies every Thursday to raise money for the church. The women, and occasionally one or two retired men, arrived at dawn to begin mixing apple filling and rolling pie dough. As soon as the pies were fried, cooled and wrapped in waxed paper sandwich bags, more volunteers arrived to deliver them to factories and businesses.*

*During the summers, my mother, the late Myrtle Wiseman, was one of the first to arrive with her three children in tow. There were a few chores children were allowed to do, but mostly we played in the church parking lot and ate our fill of fried apple pies.*

*The recipe the church used called for pounds of flour and sugar, but this is the recipe my mother used for making fried apple pies at home.*

5 cups all-purpose flour

1/2 cup sugar

2 eggs

5-ounce can evaporated milk

1/4 cup shortening

2 teaspoons baking powder

1 teaspoon salt

1 teaspoon vanilla extract

2 cups cooked apples

Combine all of the ingredients except the apples and form a dough. Pinch off a small ball of the dough and roll thin. Cut the dough into rounds using a saucer. Place 1 or 2 tablespoons of cooked apples on 1/2 of each circle. Moisten the edges of the dough using a small amount of evaporated milk, water or milk. Fold the dough over and press the edges together using floured fork tines. Continue making pies until all the dough is used.

Fry the pies in hot oil until the edges start to brown on each side.

# margaret's blackberry cobbler

*My sister-in-law Margaret Wiseman got this recipe from her mother, Ruth Markin of Ironton, Ohio, but Margaret made a few modifications.*

2 cups fresh blackberries

1 cup all-purpose flour

1 1/2 cups sugar, divided

1 teaspoon baking powder

1 stick butter, melted

1/2 cup milk

1/2 teaspoon vanilla extract

1/2 cup hot water

Place the blackberries in the bottom of a 9-inch square baking pan. Combine the flour, 1/2 cup sugar, baking powder, butter, milk and vanilla extract in a bowl and pour over the blackberries. Combine the remaining 1 cup sugar and hot water in a small bowl and stir to dissolve the sugar. Pour over the flour mixture. Bake at 350 degrees for about 45 minutes. Makes 4 to 6 servings.

# oldham pie

*Walter and Leaudra Kern, of Kern's Kitchen Inc. in Louisville, created the trademarked Derby-Pie in 1954 as the specialty pastry of Melrose Inn in Prospect. Legend has it that Oldham pie is the original recipe and that it came from Leaudra Kern, who shared it with her homemaker friends many years ago. The name might have been changed, but cooks in the area claim to have the original recipe. Here's that recipe.*

1/4 cup margarine (not butter)

1 cup sugar

3 eggs

3/4 cup light corn syrup

1/4 teaspoon salt

1 teaspoon vanilla extract

1/2 cup chocolate chips

1/2 cup chopped black walnuts

2 tablespoons bourbon

9-inch unbaked pie crust

Cream the margarine. Add the sugar and beat on medium speed using an electric mixer. Add the eggs, corn syrup, salt and vanilla extract; mix well. Add the chocolate chips, walnuts and bourbon. Pour the mixture into the pie crust. Bake at 350 degrees for 45 minutes. Serve warm with whipped cream.

# ale-8-one pound cake

*You can spot Winchester natives by the way they carry their icy cold Ale-8-One bottles – by the neck.*

*G.L. Wainscott started the Ale-8-One soft drink company in 1902. For decades it was sold only in Winchester, where it was bottled. Clark Countians who moved away asked relatives to ship cartons of Ale-8-One all over the United States and to other parts of the world. An Ale-8-One could soothe the soul when they were homesick.*

*Ale-8-One was only for drinking until we came across a recipe in the mid-'80s for 7-Up cake. It was from an African-American cook who worked for a horse farm, and she made the cake for Derby guests. It was a wonderfully moist and rich cake, and we decided it could be even better if made with Ale-8-One.*

2 sticks butter

1/2 cup vegetable shortening

3 cups sugar

5 eggs

1 teaspoon lemon extract

3 cups all-purpose flour

7 ounces Ale-8-One

Cream the butter, shortening and sugar in a bowl. Add the eggs, one at a time, beating well after each addition. Add the lemon extract. Add the flour and Ale-8-One, alternately, beating after each addition. Pour the batter into a greased and floured tube pan. Bake at 300 degrees for 1 1/2 hours or until cake tests done. Let cool in pan 10 minutes before turning out onto a cake plate.

# blueberry buckle

*Trudie and Dana Reed, owners of Reed Valley Orchard in Bourbon and Harrison counties, have 120 acres and 3,000 fruit trees that produce apples, Asian pears, blueberries, black raspberries and blackberries.*

*Trudie says her favorite way to use blueberries is in blueberry buckle, a recipe "from a dear sweet aunt, Gram Hamilton, from St. Thomaston, Maine. She was a wonderful influence on us, a great cook and mentor."*

## TOPPING:

1/2 cup sugar

1/3 cup all-purpose flour

1/2 teaspoon cinnamon

## BATTER:

2 cups sifted all-purpose flour

2 teaspoons baking powder

1/4 teaspoon salt

1/2 cup butter (1/4 cup softened,
   1/4 cup melted)

3/4 cup sugar

1 egg, beaten

1/4 teaspoon vanilla extract

1/2 cup milk

2 cups fresh blueberries, washed
   and stemmed

Combine all of the topping ingredients in a bowl and set aside.

Preheat the oven to 375 degrees. Sift the flour, baking powder and salt in a mixing bowl and set aside. Cream the softened butter and sugar in a separate bowl. Blend in the egg, vanilla extract and milk. Add the dry ingredients to the egg mixture and stir until well-blended. Fold in the blueberries. Pour the batter into a greased and floured 9x9-inch baking pan. Sprinkle with the topping and drizzle with the melted butter. Bake for 35 minutes.

# peppermint crunch

*You can have candy in a flash for last-minute gift giving if you have a pound or two of white and dark chocolate in the pantry.*

1 pound vanilla almond bark coating

1/2 cup crushed peppermint candy

Line a 15 1/2x10 1/2-inch jellyroll pan with non-stick aluminum foil. Break the white chocolate into 1-inch pieces in a 1 1/2-quart microwave-safe bowl. Microwave on high for 1 to 2 minutes or until melted. Stir until smooth. Add the peppermint candy and stir. Spread the mixture into the pan. Refrigerate. Cut or break into pieces when firm. Makes about 24 pieces.

# tiger butter

*Tiger butter was a winner in a recipe contest sponsored by the Herald-Leader in the 1980s. This is a fun recipe to make with children.*

1 pound vanilla almond bark coating
1/2 cup chunky peanut butter
1 cup semisweet chocolate morsels

Line a 15 1/2x10 1/2-inch jellyroll pan with non-stick aluminum foil. Break the white chocolate into 1-inch pieces in a 1 1/2-quart microwave-safe bowl. Microwave on high for 1 to 2 minutes or until melted. Stir until smooth. Add the peanut butter and microwave on high for 2 minutes or until melted. Stir until smooth. Microwave an additional 30 seconds if needed. Spread the mixture into the pan.

Melt the chocolate morsels, in a 2-cup microwave-safe measuring cup, on high for 1 to 2 minutes. Pour the melted chocolate over the peanut butter mixture and swirl through with a knife. Makes about 24 pieces.

Note: The peanut butter may be omitted. The dark chocolate may be swirled into the white chocolate for another variation.

# special cream candy

*My father-in-law, Russell Kelly Thompson, was born in Mount Sterling. When he graduated from high school in 1939, his first job was at Ruth Hunt Candy Co. on West Main Street.*

*He worked for Ruth Tharp Hunt, who started the company about 10 years earlier in her home on Richmond Avenue. Mrs. Hunt and her friends made cream candy after their bridge games, and it became so popular she began to sell it. She made it in her home kitchen, packing "pulled" cream candy in hand-decorated coffee*

tins, for about 10 years before opening a factory. There the candy is made in large copper kettles and is pulled and cut on an old-fashioned machine.

The company is noted for its Blue Monday candy bar. Mrs. Hunt's daughter Emily Tilghman Hunt Peck said her mother was thinking about making a candy bar and that the name came to her during church services. "She and Father went to church services one Sunday, and they had a visiting minister. During his sermon he said, 'Every blue Monday I go to the candy store and get a little sweet.' So she said, 'That's the name of the candy bar.'"

The Blue Monday is Mrs. Hunt's original cream candy covered in chocolate. Here is one of the first cream candy recipes Mrs. Hunt used. It was included in a small cookbook she wrote in 1924. The recipe has been changed slightly for today's cooks.

3 cups water

8 cups sugar

2 cups heavy cream

1/8 teaspoon baking soda

1/4 cup butter

1/2 teaspoon salt

1 teaspoon vanilla extract

Pour the water into a 3-gallon pot and bring to a boil. Add the sugar, cream and baking soda and cook until reduced by half. Add the butter and salt and cook until the mixture reaches 260 degrees on a candy thermometer. Remove from the heat and pour onto a cold, greased marble slab.

Drizzle the vanilla extract over the candy. Pull the cold candy back and forth, like taffy, for 20 minutes. Return to the marble slab and cut into bite-size pieces. The candy is very chewy at first, and then it becomes very creamy.

Note: High humidity during the candy-making process can have an adverse affect on the outcome.

# bourbon balls

*The bourbon ball is a Kentucky original, created at Rebecca Ruth Candy Factory in Frankfort. According to the company, the idea of mixing together candy and bourbon came in a roundabout way from a Frankfort dignitary in 1936. He said the two best tastes in the world were Ruth Hanly Booe's candies and fine Kentucky bourbon. Booe worked on the recipe for two years before perfecting the process for blending bourbon and candy.*

*Other candy companies and home cooks make bourbon balls, but the recipe for Rebecca Ruth Candy's version remains a secret.*

*This is an easy recipe that novice cooks use at Christmastime for gift-giving. It calls for purchased chocolate candy melts, but experienced cooks combine semisweet chocolate and paraffin for better quality.*

1 cup chopped pecans

4 tablespoons bourbon

1 stick butter, softened

1 pound powdered sugar

14-ounce package chocolate-flavored candy melts

Combine the pecans and bourbon in a bowl. Refrigerate, to allow the flavors to blend, for 3 hours or overnight. Cream the butter and powdered sugar using an electric mixer. Add the pecan mixture. Roll the mixture into small balls and chill. Melt the candy melts in the microwave according to the package directions. Dip the balls in the melted chocolate using a fork. Place the balls on waxed paper to harden. Top each candy with a pecan half while the chocolate is still wet.

# woodford pudding

*Woodford pudding is a Kentucky dish that's closely related to an old English jam pudding. This recipe was from Judge H.H. Tye of Williamsburg and appeared in the early cookbook, Out of Kentucky Kitchens by Marion Flexner.*

1/2 cup softened butter or margarine

1 cup sugar

3 eggs, separated

1 1/2 cups blackberry jam

1 cup all-purpose flour

2 teaspoons baking powder

1 teaspoon cinnamon

1/2 teaspoon nutmeg

1/4 teaspoon cloves

1 cup milk

Cream the butter and sugar in a bowl. Add the egg yolks and blackberry jam. Sift the flour, baking powder and spices in a separate bowl. Add the milk and butter mixture, alternately, to the flour mixture. Beat egg whites into stiff peaks. Fold in the egg whites. Pour into a greased 9x9-inch baking dish. Bake at 375 degrees for 30 to 45 minutes or until pudding sets. Serve hot with pudding sauce. Makes 6 servings.

## SAUCE FOR WOODFORD PUDDING

1/4 cup softened butter

1/2 cup sugar

1 egg, well-beaten

1/4 cup brandy or whiskey or to taste

Cream the butter and sugar in a bowl. Add the egg. Pour into the top of a double boiler and cook, stirring until the mixture thickens. Do not allow the mixture to boil. Add the brandy or whiskey. Serve at once with pudding.

# bourbon fudge cake

*Bourbon is as common as vanilla for flavoring cakes, pies and puddings in Kentucky. When a dinner or Derby party calls for a special dessert, here's one that's a winner every time.*

2 teaspoons unsweetened cocoa

1 3/4 cups water

2 teaspoons instant espresso

1/4 cup bourbon

5 ounces unsweetened chocolate, chopped

2 sticks unsalted butter, cut into small pieces and softened

2 cups sugar

2 cups all-purpose flour

1 teaspoon baking soda

Dash of salt

2 large eggs, at room temperature

1 teaspoon vanilla extract

Preheat the oven to 275 degrees. Coat a 12-cup Bundt pan and dust with the unsweetened cocoa. Remove excess cocoa and set aside.

Combine the water, instant espresso and bourbon in a medium-size heavy saucepan. Simmer over low heat for 3 minutes. Add the chocolate and butter; cook over moderate heat, stirring until the mixture is melted and smooth. Remove from the heat. Add the sugar and stir until well-blended. Let cool for 3 minutes.

Transfer the chocolate mixture to a large bowl. Combine the flour, baking soda and salt in a small bowl. Add the flour mixture, 1/2 cup at a time, to the chocolate mixture using an electric mixer on medium speed. Continue to beat for 1 minute after all of the flour has been added. Beat in the eggs one at a time. Add the vanilla extract and mix until smooth. The batter will be thin.

Pour the batter into the Bundt pan. Bake for 80 to 90 minutes or until a cake tester inserted in the cake comes out clean and the cake pulls away from the sides of pan. Cool in the pan on a rack for 20 minutes. Invert the cake onto the rack, remove the pan and cool completely. Serve at room temperature. Makes 12 servings.

# index

## Desserts

## Entrées

## Salads

## Sides

## Soups

Sharon Thompson has been the food writer for the *Lexington Herald-Leader* for more than 30 years. She learned to appreciate planting a garden, picking blackberries and canning pickles while growing up in rural Clark County. She attributes her cooking skills to years of interviewing the finest chefs and home cooks in the Bluegrass.

Sharon is co-author, with the late Wayne Shumate of Paris, of *Recipes From a Kentucky Blackberry Patch.*

She lives in Lexington with her husband, Bob. They have two daughters, Sarah Holleran and Emily Chambers, and three wonderful grandchildren, Paul William Holleran, Jack Henry Holleran and Eliza Rae Chambers.

Sharon's food columns appear weekly at www.flavorsofkentucky.com.

Mark Cornelison has been a staff photographer at the *Lexington Herald-Leader* since 1994. His specialties are sports – he has shot 16 Kentucky Derby winners and the 2006 Super Bowl - and musicians – his subjects have included Bruce Springsteen and John Mellencamp.

A Louisville native, he lives in Lexington with his two dogs, Jack, a golden retriever, and Abby, a basset hound.

This is the first time that Cornelison, a self-described picky eater, has taken on a cookbook. He especially enjoyed shooting pictures of the blueberry buckle on Page 140, partly because it photographed so well, but mainly because it tasted so good.